Half

MOON

Day

SUN–

The proposed dimensions of
the book are
eight by *seven* by **z**.

Composed *In* part
by concrete, black tape
and maps; string. In places,
moss, sagebrush & dill root.

FOR

My Mother,
    Maria,

& Madge, und Mai

The book acknowledging:

Many drawers at the catalogue of UWM Geographical Information Society, across a fine wing, with `listserv` & `mapsL`, at the time. And a desk there used.

Welcomeness from any place I have ever been.

Something about W. A. Mozart's "Lullaby".

My whole family.

Books about understanding roots, time, and root systems.

Alyssa for always finding a way for us.

Herb Ralph. Jan, Billu, Lotti, Franzi, a few Grahams from many ponds. James. Pat Theriault, Fransix Thevine.

Alex & Cris, anon you spring of dreams.

To the concept "The Means [Wear] By"
and Body Learning (*Gelb*). Jacklyn Maddux, thank you that Saturday a January.

Jeremy Hutchings.

The Gatzows and their gardens.

Ambits and ghosts.

Jason, Don R.,, David. Joe Bonelli, Justin, Tony & Matt and Phil. Cindy, Kendria.

Very special thanks to Abhijeet Sathe *in*
translating a catalytic poem of this book to Hindi.

Andy M.; Henk; Susan W. & A.

Kismet.

Visual orchestrations in
the poem "Lowland Spice:
Indigo, Puce, Periwinkle"
attributed to the copious
artist, wanderer, musician,
soothsayer and delicate,
time-bending soul, Al Post.
I think he's around here
somewhere.

–

M. Pinaud, thank you for
always listening and through
that engendering un-forseen
balance of composition over
our trading music, while the
project readied and reified for
distribution.

–

The number mentioned in the
poem "An Ambling Odd
Piece of Math" is fit only

forth by an entry (or example) in *Brian Greene*'s text `Until the End of Time`.

+

Some objects set in print are found from Old Book Illustrations, usable through \ *via* domain open to the public.

+

Zalex and Neera.

+

This book is best read beneath natural light.

Joshua

DAVID

Lickteig

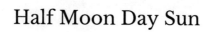

Half Moon Day Sun

Icebergs don't bother with the wind.

— David Benson

I.

C   E   E

O   R   T

V   L   S

II.

SQUARES

III.

<pre>
F   L   T

S   O   T

L   F   C

         T

         R
</pre>

Coverlets

Even a spider has gone a trio of bear's dens waiting for the night again, squaws of the blue bird beside the sand-stone clock.

Around you

You are found
It is *part* of this

Skin. This is how my skin feels. Veins
These are how my veins veil. Feet,
My feet feel the sand. Sand. This
Is how my feet feel. Feel this,
And feel that. Many things to freely
Feel. Inhale. I inhale air. Air is
Inside me. My skin breathes. I see my
Veins in my hand. My hand
Feels my blood. The body pumps
Me forward, my arms lifting
In the air. The rain
At a 90 degree angle. There again
Is the rain, as I remember. I smile
And I see my eyes. I remember my
Smile. My eyes make sounds,
      When I blink them through, like rain.

SKIN

The wheel
It would have been lost without us

Inextirpable

Simulations of a dark monsoon
Middle night seven degrees aslant

The reamer beneath
That alpine, the wheel's coverlet stashed
Out of sight.

C. 0

○

Sometime dreams are so wild,
    So tactile, so real
    The Earth falls silent
    In eerie quell of listening
    Itself.
    We walk on the floor
    And there is no sound.
    A train in the distance merges
    With the rain.
    Trumpets of crickets and creeks
    In the wind,
    Ponds and their lights
    Glimmer in the trees.

COVERTLET

[C(t).]

It was a field dream and we looked
for plants, sheep

Tides of ascending horns, the moon
 Viewing us:

Her peek shows eight views,
Prompting our bodes toward this
ink.

A, B, Y

From a memory of the trees
bridges of sun in mud
metallic bee on rose
in circles collate the barrows,
a little jade in the end

Breaking the bark of the mulberry
As a magnet placed in the moment
A refrigerator shuttered and

Candles shall stand tall as buildings
Every day you have your health
Singing bell in the left hand

Never goes out
Everything is sacred
Tarragon, red saffron — new city

A rug is born in absolution, magnet-like,
is firm after rains, of dusty when dry

The ability to fold things

MAGENTA

Ponderosa pine,
sequoia giganteum,
wild ginger,   +
hollie berries.

Basalt, andesite
    Obsidian.

"It didn't go anything as planned," he said. "I brought notes, old letters, books of art, unfinished writings.. All of it went untouched." There were two creases in each one of my good pants, and uncommon folds in my ties; shoes and boots had fallen apart in some cases, suitcoats were preserved. Maps from the library, discards, were crumpled unfittingly after not being used for fire in Ohio that evening. The tent was singed in one corner, a hole, as it was shaken over the fire to dry, the flames running into the mouthside (it was packed in wet, and stayed that way, from Mohawk hitherto).

C. 3

○

When I arrived I found no other person around the hut.
A blue candle-lighter lay by a rosily channeled fresh cut
stump. A big fog culminating from each direction: Only
an ounce or two did I see from this mount, in the last of
all the afternoon's visible, of a behemoth crag in implicit
throne east & north, over folds of v a l̲l̲ e y s and pastoral
pine after pastoral pine after pastoral pine. Inside the hut
a propane fireplace control whirs edgewise grey wavering
tones, which mistake themselves at first for other things.
There by the hut's entry-side window I found good
printed notes about the control and the fireplace's
thermostat (which was off) and its override (bypass
timer); surprise & joy had kept this rolling fire and ice
released its items, unpacked, and stripped from its wet
layers while the timer continued, overrode only the last
hour or so. My patrol is corn, a small onion, two bananas,
a jalepeño, avocado, carrot, tomatoes and orange, and an
old oat bread. Unexpectedly, there is dry parsley by the

rusted sink. Clouds over the far ice who have swum many times places else else, did so again, unveiling ashed land and a fork split the pulp to palta, claiming mix-ins of black pepper and slices of the onion moon. The bright long table and the fire.

AFTER
STROMATOLITES

If that's **eight** hours we call it nine.
I feel like there are **six** stretches.
There are **four** major joints
In the arm. **One** before none (or
No one). It only works some places.
Soften in relation to the instrument.
Undo, not correct, to give attention.
Softening our relationship with the
World. Obviate like re-inventing
One, the number, was another
Number, whose other number was

ONE

DOT

have *some of*

the good water

you poured

A bee, cat & doctor enter five gales.
How ices jut kept long masterful nature.

On paper, queues ring silently, trespassing
Under vowels. Wielding +'s yesterday zips.

A, B, Z

Milwaukee to Sault Ste. Marie

Through Sudbury to Ottawa,

To Montreal, Quebec, Saguenay

And Chicoutimi, Rivière-du-Loup,

Ste. Anne-des-Monts, Percé

And Caraquet, Charlottetown   (*P.E.I* / *I.P.E*)

New Islands & Caribou, Aberdeen ⁻⁻⁻ Gamp Abbey _

 Meat Cove and North Sydney

Channel-Port-aux-Basques to   (*Unk*)

 Corner Brook, . .

At 6:30 depart Baker to

Hell's Canyon.

PERGOLA

                    only out of the side
of my eye
          a
                                            button *on*
              a **nail**

just as

  those new seeds have a

life

     of

         their own by the wind

Fairest morning church commander deliver
namely **People** like to stay close to eachother

Snow is a reminder, lakes a cast ovum and womb of the
moons When 'mid dark foliage

Shadows uplifted slumberous lake of sea,
flowers stand meadows in ancient light.

A vastness in all of your will to be. We are types of
intervention. Laughing at the leaves

Falling. A city always. Hounds, hares. Stumps are fair.

The skin of the queen looks
like the the light of the moon. Moonlight.

SHIFT

Stumps are fair.

Tock - torch - beach - *besailed*
Our missing mastadon's licks
Mayan tryst or manic knob,
Any of our eyes blown
Into glass.

GUM BAY

How the same death *is to memory.*

Is it possible to fall through the air
no bed floor nor chair
A grasshopper made of grass
only separated by time
And sleep on the way there?

Whether it's sensitive or whether it's pain
A tenth of the rainbow's facts will explain.

C. 53

We are afraid of the ways that others
  Organize stars,

    "Out of time"

There were pictures [
        In cases where this **echo** was not present it was cordial
        To note in *digitus manus* O by absolute memory
        otherwise
        The number for further recall and use; Also this tactic
        Would make where it was common in the user's mind
        They'd not actually require a correspondence via the
        number.]

        Of { *echoes* } on their **e a r s**, fleets of reconciliation that
        Were memorable or would have remained hidden
        Without us. It will look something like this (which
        You see later in this grey dale) in the end:

C. 5

As if mountains were
In a *glass*, or her counsel
These letters of pretty gardens
That roar of a crane,
Whispering in this field.

C. 1

The mind when it is walking does not have a
Resection of most thoughts, and when it feels though the
thought is to be rejected, this is observed and a general
good feeling is born. There are floods on the beach from
the past days rain. The wind seems to blow in swirls
sometimes harsh toward the east and also the the
north-east. The waves are calm, near flat in the
mid-afternoon more south where more land lies between
the lake and the bluff; earlier, farther north there were
white waves of near a half foot around noon. The water is
the warmest it has been and to most still it is very cold.
Many faces are smiling in the sun as it has been rather
grey most day hours in the week. The water moves north
on the beach. The sails on the lake are far out and have
an appearance as if a memory. A speedboat approaches a
man rowing; they each move in the same direction,
nearer the shore. There are no gulls at this part of the
beach. Kids run and jump from a lone picnic table island
into the deeply flooded part of the beach. They lay and

turn and splash with their father sitting on the bench. A ball draws slow in the direction of a buoy on the lake, eventually stopping near, as if a conversation takes place; it passes and moves far into the distance. Time is only a consequence of the events within it. The lake has taken it. The wind also moves sometimes from the north. The whiteness far beyond the boats, the clouds, is more of an idea than an object, though it is there, as the music of the bird is there, perhaps answered or the same bird.

IT TURNED TO BE A VERY
CLEAR DAY

A snow-*fl*ake goa
  is with only start and end; incessant
the

  s t e p   ʿ

s i t s there

    and Gives up [].

Sandied glass,
  pumpkin

room is thankful.

        WEATHERLETS

All of a sudden,
things get ser-
ious while

They could hear
their kitchen green
chana

As it grows, likes to find
bits of itself and those beside
to support.

COVERLET H
[*C. H.*]

We had a while
To be back in burning
Quite

Several fair-songs
Existed, *copos de nieve* in order
From node to pond,

Undifferentiated, heavy
Lifting.

C. BRIDGE-
HOUND

In the other family's oaken eye, she felt
Recompany. *B*rusque-like she'd wrought (<u>under</u>)
Without (*[*out*]*-side) querulous
Daylight or forfending day,

The calathea from the front winds
On midnight rocks passing at noon from
A landslide.

That remade canthus. Aster to
Shades in the act of
                    Remembering.

COVERLET 4

there is
meditation, and there
just plain thinking
in the dark,
or walking in thought
while forgetting thinking
though knowing it is there
and making making
making

think

and

love

ACKNOWLEDGMENT

During preparation of the text the author
referred to information contained in several
authoritative versions of memory systems
including light bindings, knots, pencil shavings,
leaves from unforeseen gifts, rocks as walls,
waves as weather-quipus,
cāsus nor cantilever,
North via South,
sentence in
semblance,
shard by mark
or oar by door.

Olive-sided hare's eyes raised on the black night roads
Of Red Bay

Like planks steamed by Basquemen,
The boat opened like a book

Roof tiles and excavations of barrel-making remains
On the small wharf, whaling stations

Encrusted with copper cauldron bits
And burnt rock from boiling blubber oil,

Burials at the northern end of Saddle Isle, nails through
The skulls

Of forgotten sailors,
Could have been a man's will

Leaving his books, a sword and octopus
Sold by the cove and fleets abandoning the coast

As the breeze makes on the star-piece
Sets the oar, oar, oar

The farm is a place
Where gargantuan meet

Could have been he doesn't feel anger or grief, he will
just re-
Build again, the bliss of these creatures.

And the fire makes bell tea
Under-door. Any where at all I suppose

Could have been black spruce planted upside-down
On the Cambrian beach, canticles of old circus levers

Or moosetracks inside a pothole eight centimeters' deep
Found fishbone beside the lake in Roddickton, where
Toby was fine he

Said would be he supposed to camp, maybe only coyotes or black huskie
Foxes, or a blue lobster carapace from June, a trio of crows

Flown in from the Trans Canada highway, maple leaf one
On the maps,

A loon at midday in your street or a minkmouse rolling
Lignons, a Coors bottlecap or a discarded cod trap by
Keels, devil's

Footsteps, a squidhound chortling at b'y and man o' man o' war
Burning change beneath the ferries' waves, sea-twine on an ugly-

Stick outside Foley's shed, a snippet of jiggingline caught 'round

The broken step toward a cove's bench, a new bench, a
yellow

Flowertop on the gazebo's ledge in Duntara, a misshapen
brim
Along the notes of yesterday's visitor pages, foghorn by
surprise on

The lighthouse premise and ghosts of light screeching
atop the
Lookout to the stationment, winter's firewood in perfect
layers anod

In stack, green windowframes deeper than pine in the
eve, or
A queer potato - "Weeds, ah, yes, maybe! Yet a charm
they dispense -",

Religious enclaves,
An Apostle who dropped an 'H'

A Northwest wind light in the morn before Mary's
showers,
Or that Nouvelle-Écosse skunk amp joint out back the
lounge in L'anse aux

Meadows, purple-toned shale and vagabonding birch
sheets, secret
Lynx tracks in the Tilting sands, day's bakeapple mushed
in the

Fingertips washed out in the waterfall, an imperial gallon
of gold
Moonshine rum (could have been mixed with iceberg ice
and Seven Up),

Twenty thousand years and two miles thick of this,
bumblebees and
Black-flies trading buzz for billow, the woodpecker
trading tree for

Telephone pole for tree and back, side by side or side by each,
Seeing where he could get the best reception, conjoint cemeteries

On the brow of Church Hill and Chapel Hill, could have been a
Snowball's throw from Top Road to Bottom Road, a fifteen degree

Angle on the council's treasure seat: "You
  Don't drink that India beer do y'?",

Signals microwaving anon Fogo fr'somewhere
  By Musgrave..
    On the 330, a wheel from
      Rocky Harbour, a gull
        O'er first King's Cove (I)
     By
  On down to second King's Cove (II),

Partridgeberry crumble or a lost bear
 At Ochre Hill, at Gander learnt
Burns was Byron was Byrne was O'Brien, Sanders
Was Saunders and so forth,
by the vocals in the wind and

The tym', trumpets.. "It's last year's calf," you have to
watch, the Big Dipper
following me again and this time behind trees, a broken
radio in old wood shop where waterwheel once made
was, spiders in my hands, you can't
miss it, it is this dark and the Milky Way is a broken shell
from a long gull dropped way beyond the sky, almost
wrong, codwire in the fire corn coves owed coronating to
That hill, you know it is only nine hundred metres they
consider it a mountain actually otherwise it is a hill,
footsteps on placard plank posts floorwise pots by old
angles and baud art ogled not by even ninety or eighty or
so living here, this living room in the house was where a
body would go not even to the cemetery they'd keep it

here not many people at all would ever be here, small
doors bent calling ceiling joists, streams and port roads
abound travelers agog glad for ocean maybe going to
stay,

Could have been saltwater in a freshwater engine, a
zipper stuck
'twixt two turquoise rained-on quilts, rust-colored
patchwork of
bins and barn parts, half-killicks and coarse orange
plastic,
spongemoss and newspaper cascades filed in this quarry,
ruby tins
floating aside the quai who echo dew chirps from plover
cousins,
granite fastening juniper buds and satellites wound in
dandelion,
short conifer charred on train spikes, toaster cable
warped upon

fringe yankee lace, tired fisherwoman waving cheerful in
a withered
convertible, fourth year Atlantic salmon re-spawning
post-
Greenland, known trees meeting unknown trees, cabbage
and
carrot shucked under crown boat prow, Basque tongue
scratched
by roam'd Scotch rhizome, mockbeggar merchants and
vertiginous
cape sediment, a baleen fin, caplin roe or the headfirst
arrows of
gannets, ice scraped from the lightkeeper's quarters and
dark soot
from oil lamps, an ascending counterweight being
cranked to the
top of the light tower, embroidery

Parlour syndesis, an intersection of rock and home's
rough-side out clapboard

skirts, stones held by ballast locker sustaining one
hundred eighty km
winds, asphalt shingles and vinyl siding, roast red
Georgian manor
scraped by flying rainscreen,

Could have been a scissor-braced frame or twisting
gulch, road
dust from unpaved roads and stone-pocketed emulsions,
brine tankers and
squid ink on your finest white suit, no sign of
bacteriophage,

Whether edgewise over the next Fold,

    "Boreas blew a heavy squall,
    Our boat was overset."

Could have been a violin's bow from Klingenthal

Rising hull I greet
  Bright of near break
    To row time
      In the
        Lap's call

Could have been a zulu panda,
Or the first frost.

Your love is a lighthouse I see through the fog,
Anywhere 't'all should be fine. The beach roared again.

"You can't miss it."

ANY WHERE AT ALL
I SUPPOSE

Squaresails

L

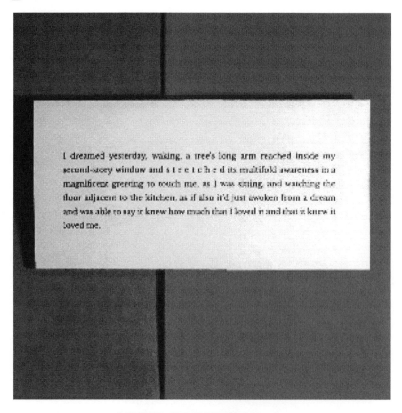

I dreamed yesterday, waking, a tree's long arm reached inside my second-story window and s t r e t c h e d its multifold awareness in a magnificent greeting to touch me, as I was sitting, and watching the floor adjacent to the kitchen, as if also it'd just awoken from a dream and was able to say it knew how much that I loved it and that it knew it loved me.

NEW GREETING, &
SQUIRRL'S MOON

NEW GREETING, &

SQUIRRL'S 2ND MOON (or,

squirrel's moon II)

Canticles, canyon. You cannot miss it.

In the *Skamania County Pioneer*,
(Single Copy 75 Cents), Volume One Hundred-
Twenty-Eight Number Seven,
Sheriff's incident log, near First ¼ moon to past
Half full moon, *lunation 1201*, "at 9:46 p.m., trees
Were reported down on the Wind
River Road near Bear Creek
Road . . ."

It is on a side of the line
Twenty duck's bills quip
ped inside or out
was a quick case of quack and quark. I saw a duck
in the stream on a hunch, like a duck from yesterday,
and from deep within it was my clearest response
to greet as if we'd just encountered each other elsewhere

Longitudes were now determined for the first time by
simultaneous

observations in both Paris and distant places, of the eclipses of the satellites of Jupiter.

LONG-BILLED CURLEW

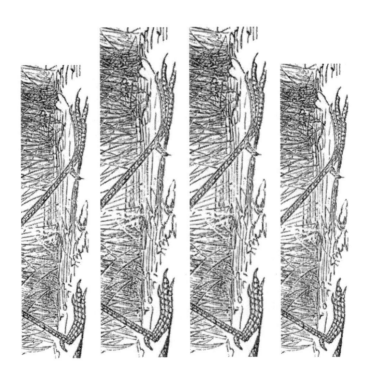

Who in India, maybe, islands ago
       invented the co-ordinated aspect
       of *1* standing (who is not
       senior) to a green sur-
       face of any inquiry
       presented on one, not
       getting lost in bone,
       articulating a sphere of math &
       devotion as it gestured
       on all of time it was
       the sanctifying tone who's invention
       that made
       the rest of everything work.

FOUR

They thought, *One* moment it wanted to build a box, or perhaps a new chair, and the next wished to reinvent *trees* or numbers.

Found an antennaed radio and
listened to organ music. Later,
listened to Koyaanisqatsi. *Find*

a blueberry muffin that
is from a bakery, after entering the
state late in the morning. The fire

warms it and the fog
coalesces with masks in the wind,
surrounding the forest. All light

will soon be, becoming lost; east
casts yestermorn's logside dust from

mount to mount to mount.

Of the edge-of-the-Earth
nights in Newfoundland and
   Labrador,

   they were not known
yet, and their friends, and
   to be *Toby*

   the abdued registers of fire
glistened
   in a forlorn lake.

Wrong cemetery
Every thing
is ghosts

In haunted zones,
idilio what

it's edges, are like

you, — garden, any-

how and *catso*und
we make a cry

O, Thy thigh
 mourn I o' marsh

FRANTIC AIR

You're not going to believe

I *am writing under candlelight*
at the cabin. I had just
invested 30 *minutes looking*
for this piece of paper.
And am *happily using my*
old desk.

The lights of the crane
become a shooting star.

At one forty-five the
  Sun
    Is southeast-south,
Walking with it is a
  Wake, even if
    Sitting, an avocado
  Heart circumscribing
With its point a
  Code in the divots
  Of rock and bird-
Crumbs, a four moun-
    Tain day, where
  The Steller's *jay's* sheet is
    Held in the wind, wet . .
      Why, it breathes, " I
feel missing"
  At eight fifty one
The sun is east.
  At eight and six minutes,
On a new morning, north-northwest

Beams arrive of lowland spice . .

The **moon** is wet,
The moon is West.

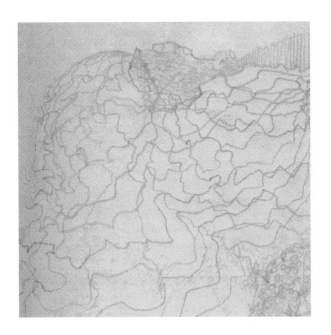

LOWLAND SPICE **i n d i g o**

The dark goes
  To light,

    Harp on passage the   ▽
  S p i d e r is

  Confused, not
Under daunt, for

A blink of an orange moment
  On a cactus. Green new growth

Very tall

        LOWLAND SPICE **p u c e**

Ten **thirty**-seven, sun is east and slightly southern,
A mirror beams a shaft north into the home,
Easterly; Another **mirror** beams
Light east and south, almost for the
Direction of the sun itself

LOWLAND SPICE p e r i w i n k l e

I N D I G O

P U C E

PERIW*I*NKLE

Open space counts,

one, <u>two</u>,
"one seventy-**five**, right
on the money:",
Light counts,
sometimes,
like five, six, nine.
Eyelashes count,
 8, seven,
sixty-five,
plant green
r**oo**ts,
when no one is

      looking.

O, OR I

After hiking **M**t. Adams in the White

mountains began west
and from the *302 (10)* from the *3*

was found to be entering a town
called Bethlehem, whom on the
blue entrance placard has a phrase:

"Poetry Capital of New Hampshire."

As the highway turns to *Main* a
small sign in chalk on the
grass leads to a final evening

in a brewery shack, before they
moved that season. Nestled fire in
brick at near-dusk, phantom talks & good knowing's
      velvets,

velvets in the sky turn to night,
the trees lay flat behind all of us.

I lusted after all of us.

           LATHE

A leap in the blue sun
of the coquí 's call
has our hour added o'er
blinking bulbs, for

Like a seed in the ears
of a *Corylus*, in fact
a kind of birch (if not
considered a horn-

Beam), asks it, *where **are** you,*
whose fruit, uncracked,
dreams in variations
of me.

LIFELIKE

To sea in
brightness

unsure how much
many of it was
before

By the salt mounds they told us
<< *es imposible pasar*
      por est_ carretera >> The land is
Private. The trucks and gears, cranes
      And motorbikes were there
         Long ago. The bandana
Of the man obfuscates his face; this pink
      Flamingo rides the pluperfect
        Waves in the wind,
And then another. Our brows are salted
      And our hats
Thick with soil of our heads and the stances
      Of the dusts and the warm
Maths of jungle and melted
Emulsions of cars, and salts;
The pink cloaks are set by A
      Sun passing again, invariable as if
        Ago and becoming..

We drove farther along, with

No tarry on heavens of
Salt we were precaution'd of, peeling oranges.

We re-ordered ourselves on a gravesand
Switchback and watched the birds,
          Looked for turtles.. Over

A dune opposite the gulf we
          Were alone with yet another
                    Class of the sea,
In the beach small bubbles edifying
          Our wake.

ORANGE

His name is Rodolfo,
Tillamook

A penny from **1974** outside of
Nap's t h r i f t w a y store

Chimney sweep, tractor tuning
From *huinca* to Beckett : :

       *   *   *   *   *

SNOW ZONE
Chains Required
When
F L A S H I N G
  *   *   *   *

EASY BEFORE
HEAL

Get the date parameters

If the year doesn't exist, create it

If the month doesn't exist , create it

If the day doesn't exist (it shouldn't) create it

Iterate over the dates and make partitions

Δ START &

Δ END

They are doing that
In the 80's
Right now,
  No snow
       Although darts
And pre-ambles of
      Fair-bridged
      Flare, cabbage-lit
 Deregulations and
Marble sample
  Swoons, sanded
      On trapeezes
  Lazy bears, taut, knitting. Secret

Before the secret
Ever existed, an
Under-topped teaspoon
Crossing origin with background radiates.

C. BOLETUS

PATA PATTERN PARA
PROTON PROGNOST—
ICATORY PORT—
ENT PON PRETEND
PREY PE PLORE
PLOMB PLU
PLUS PUT
PATH PANG
PART
PAT
P

As the day rises there are
houseboats, a language with soft
edges, a city with softest drink-
ing water and delicate sinks.

ALLE LEGENDARISCHE

for Jan Tjalling-Oosten

ALLE LEGENDARISCHE

AS THE DAY RISES, THERE ARE
HOUSEBOATS, A LANGUAGE WITH SOFT
EDGES, A CITY WITH SOFTEST DRINK-
ING WATER AND DELICATE SINKS.

THE STREETS ARE LINED WITH CINNAMON, AND THE
WALLS CAN BE BUILT ROUND WITH NINE SHADES
OF MARMORAE BRICKS FROM CLAY ALONG A
RIVER. YOU ARE IN FACT BELOW SEA-LEVEL
AND BETWIXT HUNDREDS OF BUILD-
INGS WITH THOUSANDS OF WINDOWS, MONU-
MENTAL ARRANGEMENTS AMONGST FEATURES
OF MARITIME ENGINEERING. THE SEAGULLS
ARE TALK & TINE, AND BEHIND FRENCH THE DOORS
HIDE A MULTITUDINAL SOUNDS OF FLOWING, A NO ONE AL-
MOST TELL YOU ONCE, THE DUTCH MOVING RATHER RAPID-
LY AND PEOPLE FROM MANY OTHER LANDS AND THE
SPARROWS YOU JUST RETHINKING ABOUT BEING PLACES
THEY WERE SUPPOSED TO BE. COVERINGS, PAN-

CAKE INFRAST-   EVERYTHING THE STREET   THE RISING OF
RUCTURE, FOOD   IS HALF-FREE BRANCHES   HIGH TIMES AND
TO GATHER AND   HANG VERY THROUGH SUN-   THE LIGHT BE-
THE LAND BENEATH DAYLIGHT, SEA CABLES, AND LONGING OF
ARE QUIET, ONE IM- CAREFUL PEOPLE GASLITS NARROW BUILDINGS
AGINE STILL THIN-   HISTORIES OF GRAV-   TO SAVE THEIR
KING AS WORK   ITY THROUGH THE ART   STRENGTH
EVER DOES, CLOCKS THAT DON'T KEEP TIME AND
A CURVILINEAR SUBSTRATE OF
CONNECTED TO ALL THINGS, A AWARENESS TO DELICATE
BRINGS YOU HIGH LINTELS   FUNCTIONS, CRAFTSHIP,
WITH A DAZZLING ASSORTMENT   AND DESIGN. SIMPLICITY
LARGELY AND MINUTE   AND SUSTAINED KNOW-
FURNISHINGS THAT BEING   LEDGE LAY IN FIGURE
OF NO RESERVATIONS AND EXPECTATIONS
ARE HANDLED IN PARSIMONY BY, AS A RULE,
WOULD, CAREFULLY AVOIDING THEM. AS THE DAY
SETS, WE DREAM.

This plant is a lion.
It was by design
The ontology was not
Loaded and memory
Rangered its own being
  To fault, as leaves

In panels, if the object
Lay beneath an onyx,
And other onyxes be—
  Neath this.

HAND POEM

वह चक्र
बगैर हमारे लुप्त रेहता

चक्रव्यूही

माल्हार के साये
सारथी की गीता

क्षणो से बुने कंबल
मे लिपटा अर्जुन
करे प्रतीक्षा

C. 0 (Hindi)

As legit was
a chancellor'd
making, or chance, and ship —
it was exposed that
a response was un-
chosen, acted upon,
and actually sayed.
When else was,
 ideas expected.

LATHELIKE

Cicero Ave.,
    The glimmer man

    And the pattern
    Of our fate (emdash)

    Around the mountain
    I am

    A rare birth
    Whose glimpse moves
    The valleys

    To the moutaintops,

    The seas again
    To the river.

      WHAT SAID POLONIUS?

It would have
been written evenstone
with a quaint posture,
 "Killingsworth" sign
is seen from
"*T*urn, Tu*r*n, Tu*r*n" : : in equipoise
it's only a hanging light
join'd to distinct
sparrow's gold.

APOSTLE JOIN

At the inspected despair
of captivation, as 'x'
The bell wrote sound,
told of time, in 6's;
The flea came
in from
the
sea
to the **v**eld.

one **fire** does not
make winter

The only coverlet
that has two parts
is the one finding a city —
The day's shore is
in whispers
of what takes

SHORES OF US

As You Are A *Person, You* Are *Different*

Things In *Different Places*

We have to *sneak up*

on our *reflexes.*

As if a *dowel*

between the *years.*

I can feel *the hands*

of my teachers.

(_ reprise _)

Sometimes dreams are so wild,
So tactile, so real
The **Earth** falls silent
In eerie quell of listening
Itself.
We walk on the floor
And there is no sound.
A train in the distance merges
With the rain.
Trumpets of crickets and creeks
In the wind,
Ponds and their lights
Glimmer in the trees.

That incinerate root
Of the bog, it happened
On nodes of fall:

Non-constant where
The burst on saddles

Wramped blue and cosmoid
Concurrency of ribs,

Sanded by vow of
Agog neurosynesthetes,
Trembling of new

Cants as angels burned on woe-
Born paradise,
Widdling in squat
The swizzle with
Queens in the middle,

Basalt atop
And quizzes being
      Zookeepers.

C. QUAM

PRIMUM

	A	S	T		Y	E	A	R			Thimblebe	rries
L												
	A		W	I	N	D	O	W				
W	A	S	B	R	O	K	E	N				
	&	N	D		T	H	E					
M	A	N		S	T	A	N	D	S	⊕		
	B	E	S	I	D	E		T	H	E		
G	L	A	S	S		B	Y		T	H	E	
D	O	O	R	.	W	A	S					
N	E	R	V	O	U	S	[	I	N	⊕		⊕
[	[		[	[	R]	[	[	[				
U	N		N	E	]	V	E	D				

]	]		*J*	*J*		]	]	]			
	u	n		n	e	r	v	e	d	d	⊕	.
T	H	E		MI	D	D	L	E			
C	H	E	E	K	S		S	U	P	-	
P	L	A	N	T	E	D		B	E	Y	-
O	N	D		T	H	E		S	H	A	M	E
O	F		Th	I	S		S	T	O	R	E	'	S
S	C	A	R		B	Y		T	H	E	
S	I	L	E	N	T		M	o	⊕	N	
	K	E	E	P	I	N	G		O	U	R
	O	R	A	N	G	E		T	R	A	I	T	S
S	A	F	E		A	N	D		I	N		**A**

			c	p	u		e		
			a	s	l				
N	E	W		O	R		N	E	X	T
S	H	E	L	L		O	F		U	N	D	E	R	-
S	T	A	N	D	I	N	G		T	H	E
R	E	P	A	I	R		W	A	S
	A	G	A	I	N		C	L	O	S	E	R
I	N		T	H	E		D	A	W	N	.

BEFORE WINDOW

(BEYOND *GRADUS*)

Verified the complaint. Traced
Cause of fault to shorted out-

Put device
All other components are aok.

Called and left message to call me.

Need info on what happened to
Cause this so it won't happen
Again.

It may have been caused by
Shorted wires. Pleae make
Sure customer talks

To B— when they call back. Using
The same ones bought from us.

Working aok.

REPAIR ORDER

Seventies Film and
Library Music

actually, this doesn't happen

Alackad*a*y & 0 *map*s happen,

In the **WAY** the seventies .. 7

and libraries

disappear

After as marshed
tags unset

Beside the
small plants

In the sun,
before ⊥'s breakfast

Like church: Amsterdam
one hour before the ballet,

Also a fat cat nabbling, grhisbibbling the bar
named Thomas, with

Twenty-**seven** whiskers,
Daylight nowhere near

And petroleum
blinding aggregated nostrils

From a crease in
the wall near the washroom, this

One man on a chair
talking about the disappearances

Of foam in the glass,
after lips save touches

it, on the circle:

As what drank from the
glass

It was distinctly
their ail

  Aneath but bu-
i-

Lding into, glumping, *grisbytyng* into
the substruct

Ballasts of lips,
again around

That enormous lantern
in the sea.

TOUCH

Mist from a distance

~ eight ~

een in. *Leaving no more*
residual moisture than

A natural morning dew.

NOTE 3 ON MISTING +

Plum Banania

Purple little uplifting module

Basic ancillary nested and noduled arc

Jaquefroot

**Jovial ardent cusps kinesthetically flowering
rays useful if tempered**

As garlic dive-
bombs into my plantain
soup, garrisons
witness a benign
fold of soup-forest
and vacuums whir
once on the new
moon, twice on
full, and
rooms make other
rooms

FIND SYMPHORICARPOS

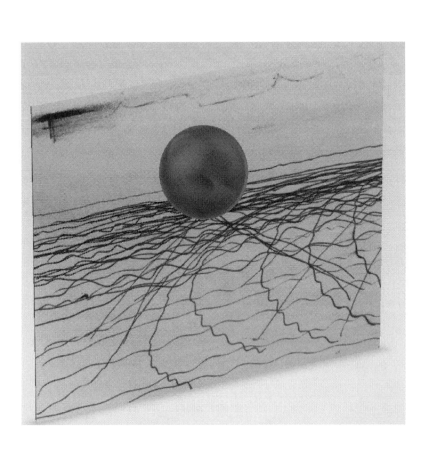

I dreamed yesterday, waking, a tree's long arm reached inside my second-story window and s t r e t c h e d its multifold awareness in a magnificent greeting to touch me, as I was sitting, and watching the floor adjacent to the kitchen, as also it'd just awoken from a dream and was able to say it knew how much that I loved it and that it knew it loved me.

A gnat perched on rim
of *añejo* tequila, lemons
rooting tendrils
of their skin amongst
indian okra

strawberry bonded to amethyst or thyme

wax swept on the sun rug

metanodes mop old leaf knowns

over promontory where

sails hugged the shore, maybe mistaking

a bay for a large river

or whatever,

print on postcards crab

to spokes in city underpasses

finest shorn streetcar linings

and old signs about the cars

while storms plan new storms,

and those animals that

know about them count reeds

to sleep

EULALIA

Chopsticks blush ashes curtain

On the registers of the mezzanine
In the garage I created a schema for prayer.
Dannl and I talked as she leaped on
An edge, showing its wear over the years.
Yes, I lost my pen at **LAX**. With the index slicing,
A versicolor truck was porting parts as the sun beamed in.
 Of course I ventured unto zap along the way: it is as if I
had been *here* twice,
 Though with or without fact I'd not been there even
once. An old TNT
Switch lay on the table behind me. Danni dan dead-
In-the-eye
Held a life vest and a seat belt in a photgraph behind her,
Wife & she beside eggplant ducks '88. If
 You look at *Purple Noon*
Early on, Alain Delon holds
 Nova Scotia,
A pencil at the
 Café like he's not held
  One afore.

yet untraceable 88

brief intermission, ⊙

please use stairs
for re-entry

boustrophedon

After a good rain, something that has been hanging for,
hm, like many hours: When the rain comes **&** then when
the next thing comes:

      *Active memory **of** function, and\or*
      regalia
      at any
      moment.

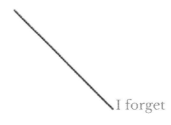

I forget

if

the intermi-
ssion

is sequence

OR

when middle

masts most
otherwise

our fuses
in the
s*u*n

yes the middle of the page begins in the end of the page

(a violin *moves)*

there could

      very well

      be an-

      other section

      to KNOW about

Space not place.

I.

The black-bird songs are in sevens and nines, the dipthongs
of their two red wings with the gull's chimes of three.
Their feet in the sand, the rabbit's eye an ampersand,
appears once, twice behind the plant.

II.

There is a spot on owe in west
Where o'er swamp doth buzz
Near the thirteen, evidently
Squirrels and raccoon combine
And the tune of the moon
Carries mattresses for hidden gobi.

III.

Wye on the route de l'Acadie
Red sands, marsh salt lands

Mi'kmaq moon on the noon-day
Sky wires to the sleuth'd
Cormorant,

Her episodes from the mists
Anon the isle are the lens of our
Hearts. A home is no voice
A voice is a blind crest, a binnacle

Westnorthwest.

SIRAJLI'S **COUNT**ERELUDE
(Beyond | Before *DOLLARD*-DES *ORMEAUX*)

The ceremony itself, delivering
Message ▯s with little
To no loss, as all of

The days-by-days feel good
It will wail for

The soonest splines
In the wind and trucks
Driving, motors binding
A round and a round

—Swains in the end of summer's ra
in,
Shipping revolutions through
the post-.

C. *of*

CONCURRENT PEAR, 2019

It is important to impart balance
Between passion & objects.

To be able not into the moment apply
New in order to progress

An idea held by a closed clue.
Where certain ideas reveal true

Vales order parley to blue insights.

GONDOLA PERGOLA GAZEBO
FINIAL PROMENADE

If 0 = dark and 10 = bright, light should

move from about 3 to 6 and back.

— Beckett, S., "Breath" (1969)

- v e /

coverlets afire in a land

locked cove

Acape of waiting,
Her quorum sensing
"We were like the ship, we

Stayed here, too."
At first it did not much feel
Like any where at all.

Beach *is*

A transition between
Sea and sand, or

              unlike
              lake and sand.

They will be induced
To leave their shell, with a shock.

I am not a string,
And nor are you. The string I

Suppose least, the tuned end
Of the axe in a bearthroat,
Abseil lowbush contra alder.

I SUPPOSE I DID, THERE
WERE NO LIGHTS
UP THERE
OR ANYTHING
LIKE THAT

+ve

Easy before heal.

As the sounds begin. Tonight
We get through all of it.

Bringing a table to the skyline.

The road is balance of the lived
and the sensed.

More order with each day.

III

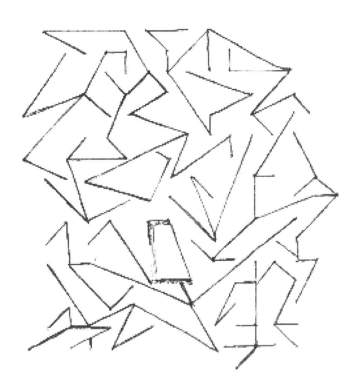

I don't believe there is *a grain.*

— Hazard, James

Flutes of the
Leafcutter

THIS
plant is

A LION

To distribute a captured image of handwritten or otherwise composed **word** packages the poem as object yielding for itself patterns of access beyond a *witnessed* spoken event or private downstream discovery from a bookshelf, **table**, yard, or rucksack. An **ant**. By the so present and also most elephan*tal* stream such images within images will hold parallel reflection of the medium itself, worth experiencing and investigating in terms of true distance from the human breath, and what we have elided alongside what we believe we find.

RELIQUARY

Think how a tiny round spider
at work in the set of sundown
casting bit on bit of the web
in the long corners of a tall
cactus as the earth turns in surprise
and shadow comes to light as if dawn
has blinked will pause with this,
re-dial the sow & nod
in compass by the curls of
bloom anew.

MORNING SPIDER
POEM

our birth is an um-
brella of our
    hope, our hope
a hop along the
petals in purple
and the plantings
    of unborn
    wonder.

SETTLING OF
MAKER'S HANDS

The field's eph —
emera was another-
er part of a sheep.

Doing so it was
left where
context roots | | | || | | fenced
its submission

In a giant esc—
ape.

C. *type* `BEAM`

In the washroom, "<u>Hugging</u>
the Shore,"

rune, squaresails and easy heal

patches of sun on concrete
plant at the door

a document merged
beneath the blankets

from three sessions of editing
over **2** years,

Madge's sketch of *El Gaucho*
by the bonsai tree.

A condor bowl, a bighorn bowl
*What is it to create a sacred **spot**?*

And where a wan danse macabre?

CARVING PUMPKINS
IN JANUARY

I am faring the Grace Sparkes
back to *Cotteyyl* island to
the eastport peninsula.

Three feet dangled unbelievably
    far from the ship
  walking also, never wound
   by organ's whispers of
    absent mirth,
          ass of themselves
    They thought — never —
     never better than *than* the
    marmot, in her dome,
     shaking berry twigs at
        the bones of ants.

VIGESIMAL

Said ' *O V L* '

rev O

the

n i a t n u o M

MOMENT

4

Often was forgotten
   steel layered above
      consonants would rei-

Fy when wisting warblers
   sent eyes on the
      geysers in extended
   dereference —

Glass not yet unborn *tapabocas*
   though at belet mime

CUPOLA

I can see the
videostone

Why are you
watching my eyes

It may ask and be
absent

VIDEOSTONE

That order is hewn
forty-five minutes warming

Up. Sun from the south and west
dockside, entropic stream

A star journey fit in
the sleeve of the pictures

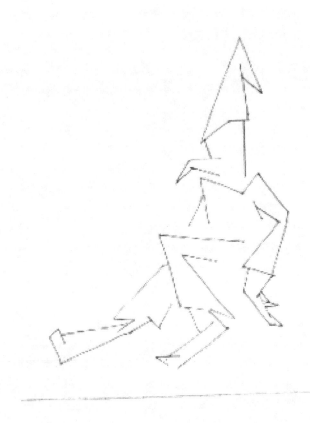

It is so easy to narrate one *Coverlet*, especially looking
At that rackled space and rails are seaweed in the gap I
see,

Previous.

C. 9

In a shroud of pendula
You gave a glimpse to me.

In the in-
dex of
legs, so

fendered
our id-
ea of

*o*utspinnings.

C. 999

Well, first, got your new address.

I did get the bit about Inova and sent a reply.

More later.

A NOTE FROM JIM

Le rocher en equilibre.

Pause

My broom sits by my guitar
On a quiet street where all goes meek

A spider watches empty picnics
In the disappeared.

A snag or gravity,
The intricate things lay hiding

Roofs, wound for tomorrows
when earth undoes earth

AND SANDS

SAVE

On the wall
in the door
a hat on the
   stove
and ads for
'Coverlet Ad
   Flustra'
shown in the
   tape register,
a key right
   below the
     edge of
   the screw,
wooden plates
   where love
wound ancient
   garages
in a mirror
on the wall.

C. *AD*

FLUSTRA

It's as if **e**'s *are being handed by root shadows to the*
tree~

That the sculptures believed
A *wrinkle* in the eye

Was twelve plus one
Eleven plus two

Be rain. Be pure, be three.

CASKET LEAF

On a **rhubarb** sailshot I knew
chrysalis, Quidi Vidi

.. from where I would in fact
see myself next

88 . . Mostly what
would become bamboo

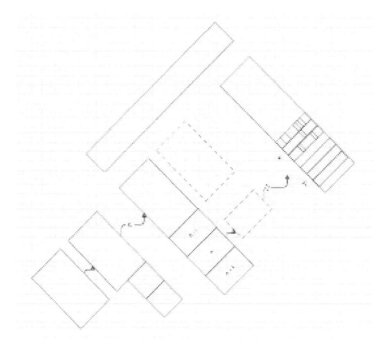

Mountain-girdling bands. *Octillion.*
Mostly what would become *periwinked.*

With one hundred two-sided stars, hanging upside or
down
the number of combinations of half

being each case are:
      100,891,344,545,564,193,334,812,497,256. Wow!

If we delimit this string of numbers
and construct two sets by collecting

it's alternate decimal groups:
      100 344 564 334 497
      891 545 193 812 256

And sum the elements of its
perpendicular planes:
                        1839
                        2697

      991 889 757 1146 753

And follow the same to another stage,
each conclusion is the same:

$$4536 \quad 4536.$$

If these are added we have 9072,
which number's base 36 (hexatridecimal)
representation is 700.

AN AMBLING ODD PIECE OF MATH

pop & prune
saw dwarfs
alder thickets
sawed wharfs

What is it, what **does** it mean,
  To be remade?

One week after the cabin burned to the ground.

Remember when:

The stars still came out.

I want you to find the "brightest star" (hint in **Canis Major**)

Sirius magnitude -1.60, 9 light years away & look !

Canopus magnitude -0.73, 650 light years away from our sun.

Rigel (winter) *magnitude -0.20, and is 540 light years*

away.

What is it to re-understand
Mostly what would become your truth.

Any moment can be filled with doubt.

That way a rug is changed on the wall,
From the floor.

thrive

I   D

X   N

LIST OF PHRASE NODES ARRANGED BY
UNENDED CIRCUMFERENCE,
sorted with an alphabet

[numbers], cf. Deut.

A

ago, ORANGE

aok, REPAIR ORDER

aleph, cf. "beginning"

alpine, COVERLET 0

ape, COVERLET *type* `BEAM`

art, *a lens or anything else mattering to perceive motion in*
   a world, or eons

architects, *pretty much left*, though in certain manners,
   designs remain unencumbered

aspect, see *horse*, see also *"seahorse"*

"[a] bee", A, B, Z

B

basalt, COVERLET (QUAM PRIMUM) ; interlude ;
   ocean rock ; basis on balanced

table in reference via . . *La roche equilibre*
Basque(*s*, [sic], *coll.*) (of Labrador, <u>Nfld.</u>), (fmly.
LUMBERED, <u>PERGOLA,</u> ->
pangola, also, sets of mandolin, perhaps)
bats, but *see* entry, "xenon"
be, *var.*
bee, A, B, Z ; ANY WHERE AT ALL ..
bean(s), *see* legumes and their sisters, chana dal (*green*)
behindrance, REGISTER
beneath, [book's entry\acknw.] ; C. 0 ; ANY WHERE
        AT ALL I .. ; HAND POEM ; CARVING
        PUMPKINS IN JANUARY ; *mucus* ; epilogia
bog, IT WAS THERE & IT WAS .. ; COVERLET
        (QUAM PRIMUM)
bookshelf, RELIQUARY
blood, SKIN
blouse, IT WAS THERE & IT WAS ..
blue, LIFELIKE
bluejay [sic.], *Mostly after April for some time, in to early*
        summer as I remember there; afterward assumably
        preferring westerly roosts from Balch crk.
        "long-crested, mountain, or pine jay"; very
        "Mot-Mot", look near temple by Bacalar
bonsai, CARVING PUMPKINS IN JANUARY
broom, AND SANDS SAVE

C

cactus, *cf.* `semi-cactus, or deeply unforlorned
bird-chime`, "tomato cactus" ; *Euphorbia [..]* or
Euphorbia ingens on a Sunday, carried from
Burnside St., 20th *to* Upshur, by forest ;
MORNING SPIDER POEM ; *cf. also*, latex
caduceus, (cf. *Hermes*, "contiguation"), also, determine
bands like B52's; but meaning mostly *help*
candle, *As lighted, it's reflection is seen in a car window,*
long from the counter it sits on, and from that
window another, perhaps several as night shifts
photons ; (*var.* candle-lighter), AFTER
STROMATOLITES (*estromatolitos*) ; (*var.*
candlelight), *somewhat foreseen* (either title or
semi-interlude page) ; outside right now ;
Also, have you had this mystery of: You had a
candle lit for some hours, and then you are
ready to move to another thing and you
extinguish it with a breath, and you move to
the other thing, but then .. you find yourself
in a circumstance to have the candle lit
again!, and you walk in the dark to it while
also finding a way to light it - you find the
way - and you tip the candle to ignite, and O*!*

cranes, ORANGE

creativ (-eness, -ity), *it remembers something on this* ;
Would be seen again ; *always played well in either individual or group circumstances* ; "could not bounce ball"

D

death, *Coverlets*

devil's root, *Missa for your brilliance*

dew, NOTE 3 ON MISTING

dipthong(s), SIRAJLI'S COUNTERLUDE

dowel, *As You Are A Person You Are Different . .*

dream, NEW GREETING, AND SQUIRRL'S MOON

E

eggs, IT WAS THERE & IT WAS .. ; "Robin's Egg
Blue" (*unprinted anywhere though oft part to a chime in abstruse reconciliations*)

endless, *Nameless* ; hearts

estromatolitos, AFTER STROMATOLITES ; ORANGE

everyday, see *Epilogue*

ex, X, *XX*

F

faucet, *will not turn the volume up for your music finding*

a time, Can be done with watch or looking
into distant direction for indicator as to
where it was
forest, IT WAS THERE & IT WAS ..
foil, *folded like an eight*
flutes, *Remind self of flutes, flute-cutters, stream-cutters,*
and leafs ; cf. III. Flutes of the Leafcutter

G
gazebo('s), ANY WHERE AT ALL I SUPPOSE ;
(intermission)
ghostberry *(colloquial)*, FIND SYMPHORICARPOS
gnat(s), IT WAS THERE & IT WAS .. ; (either title or
semi-interlude page)
gobi, SIRAJLI'S COUNTERLUDE, *cf. Neera* (circa
D.D.O., Quebec ; also, thank you Pat)
gravesand, ORANGE
gravity, AND SANDS SAVE, *also many S's moving*
toward un-"S"-*like* things levitating where
you'd least expect (the) greatest thing you
ever did, . . . *our fuses \ in the \ sun*
green, COVERLET (QUAM PRIMUM)

H
½ moon day sun, **HALF MOON DAY SUN**

haunted, FRANTIC AIR

hematosis, see *something like*, "manner of the
        irreverent street bicyclist" (`Ten
        Control Mills`, `iTopia` [Russell, D.]), *though not*
        within a poem but physically deconstructing into a
        single thing / filtered manifest by way of a tumble
        on Mississippi Avenue, NE

Hindi, COVERLET 0 (*translation, fl. Abhijeet S.*),
        around p. 100 in unmarked paginated book

[**Hh**]uinca, A play produced by Teatro Milagro in
2019,
        written by Marilo Nuñez ;
        see also *Mapuche* word in oral tradition of
        Chile, sometimes meaning "thief", or
        "outsider" ; EASY BEFORE HEAL

houses in the 80's, in Wisconsin, with like 19 VHS

I

India, FOUR ; *2005* ; cf. also Sukhwinder

inextirpable, COVERLET 0 ; *neologism*

"**intermission**", which sometimes says to itself,
        there may be intermissions of inter-
        missions.

ISBN, [cf. ISBN] ; *Wait, did you mean `Ibsen`? ; . .*
Another

wait, did you mean `It's been?` I honestly can't say
— let's try and figure this out another time. I'm
fine with that. ; *Reflects and re-reflects general*
uncertainty about the Library of Congress, again,
anyhow.
IRREFERENCEABLE, *see inline title about 2-L, spelled*
out with an alphabet, possibly referenced for
indexing ; also, *think about* the alphabet

imposible (Esp.), ORANGE (**line following has ambiguous*
determiner)
italicized semicolon (*decisions about*), *ibid.*

J
jungle, ORANGE
joy [], remember about *"this is the way, step*
inside"

K
kitchen, NEW GREETING, AND SQUIRRL'S MOON
; COVERLET H ; *null*
Koyaanisqatsi, *see* Glass, P.

L
land, ORANGE

lazy, C. BOLETUS

lemonseeds, *Yes, O they rush with me*

lathe, That night, slept in Robert Frost's backyard

M

magenta (color), *see* available schema from 1990's
        video games, early ;

MAGENTA ; colors moving *f/* early stare to later stare
        (*l e t   u s   l e t   t h e   f o r e s t   d e c i d e*)

many, SKIN

Mahendra, THIS PLANT IS A LION

matinée, *no found reference though something may have*
        taken place

Maya, GUM BAY ; ORANGE ; sometimes a space,
        sometime not ; calendar often confused with
        those from Aztlan

meniscus (of vodka, beside a resting fork, or upturned
        rock), *not here, though look for the point of the*
        foxes, maelstrom of delivery in a group of heads
        which is very loving & similar to a long round
        table and all of it's interactions, and chaws and
        clicks of intimate elements and foundry of the
        crow's throat.

Mi'kmaq, DOLLARD-DES ORMEAUX, (i.a. Sirajli's
        Counterlude)

Milwaukee, PERGOLA, (*fmly.* LUMBERED)
Milwaukie, *rhododendron*
monsoon, COVERLET 0
moon.,
mound, ORANGE
mucus, see *mucielage* or *cloth* ; [once per every year]
        see *blood,* or *whisps* ; see also *hapless humours,*
        or eggplant welcoming, beneath a 'moon day
        mucus sun'
multifold, NEW GREETING, AND SQUIRRL'S
        MOON [*sic*]

N
nabla, *harp* (inverted Greek delta) ; LOWLAND SPICE
        [puce]
narration (of 'Coverlets'), C. 9 ; RELIQUARY
        necessary things that have been read over
        time, *What find for having read this?*
neurosynesthetes, COVERLET (QUAM PRIMUM)
nematodes, see *metanodes*
Newfoundland (NL, Nfld.) & Labrador, (provinces) an
        interlude ; *2017* ; PERGOLA ; first reads on
        ANY-WHERE AT ALL I SUPPOSE
nineteen-todays, *Day with nineteen days*
nitrogen, *please see* legumes & make friends with fixers

of them, i.e. being in the soil :), wait is that an
    `emoji`, mostly don't having find them lol ?
noon, IT TURNED TO BE A VERY CLEAR DAY ;
    SIRAJLI'S COUNTERLUDE ; COVERLET 4
90° angle, SKIN ; boxes

O

Ohio, COVERLET 3 ; *not without tent-patching, and a*
    vast small fire burned your edges
108, *46min* remaining (to print) ; now less than that
orange(s), ORANGE ; AFTER STROMATOLITES
    (*estromatolitos*)
Oregon moss, *see* streams and rockbeds, also fixtures
    by sea
ossicones, *for Squindl*
ourselves, ORANGE
outspinnings, COVERLET 999
ovules, *see* (unmade) The Snow Is Moon
owl, REGISTER

P

petals, SETTLING OF MAKER'S HANDS
pear (concurrent), *That thing just doesn't know where to*
    go
pink, ORANGE

plants (being lions), HAND POEM
pluperfect(*ion*), ORANGE
polygonal kangaroos, *a new painting it will live there*
Portland, Ore., *Si*
posture, APOSTLE JOIN
picnic, AND SANDS SAVE
printed, *unforeseen circumstance* (either title or
      semi-interlude page)
+ *plus*, A, B, Z ; Acknowledgments ; *Mai's Fire* ; (+ v)
puce, LOWLAND SPICE
purple, SETTLING OF MAKER'S HANDS ; ANY
      WHERE AT ALL I SUPPOSE ; yet
      untraceable '88
Puyanawa, λόγος

Q
Qidi Vidi, AN AMBLING ODD PIECE OF MATH
Quebec, PERGOLA
queen(s), COVERLET (QUAM PRIMUM)
(of) quack and quark, LONG-BILLED CURLEW
q u e l l (*to*), MAGENTA
queue, [transaction lost]

R
rain, SKIN

ratchet(s), *cf.* "bluejay"

record, *Flip it now, though wait for it, work on something,*
        and then, put it on again

"regular expression", *see 'moss' &c., as just in garden*
        commits new edges to itself

remember, SKIN

Rodolfo (a variegated albino tree squirrel), EASY
        BEFORE HEAL ; *circa idem tempus, (*C.R., *2017)*

root(s), IT WAS THERE & IT WAS .. ; COVERLET
        (QUAM PRIMUM) ; COVERLET *type* `BEAM`

rucksack, RELIQUARY

S

saddles, COVERLET (QUAM PRIMUM)

salt, ORANGE *(cf. Mx.)* ; SIRAJLI'S COUNTERLUDE

schefflera, A *day in early summer, from the local*
hardware
        store. Likes leaves washed in the tub and then
        afterwards gleams listening to other trees and a
        nodding forest sun.

sea, ORANGE

seven(s), *[°]* COVERLET 0 ; (as planned numerical
        dimension) ; *"twenty-seven whiskers"*, TOUCH
        ; *black-bird songs*

sheep, COVERLET *type* `BEAM` ; A, B, Y

shell, *mostly arranged in patterns of moose* ; beginnings

simulation(s), COVERLET 0

shoes, COVERLET 3

sixteen control mills, *different book*

skin, SKIN

sleep, *Itself came from a delirium?* ; EULALIA

"softs", (*invented*, likely f. *"tooths"* + Something like:
    "My soft", Shakesp., *see directly* Venus and
    Adonis space, [one before each indexed entry
    within character- or symbol- 's dimension]

spill, *appreciate the wave, or it's timing, & and a*
    revelation to the unknown

s q u a r e s a i l s , *T*, &II., *and most for* <u>*inflatons*</u>

[squirrel(s)], cf. NEW GREETING .. ; little claws ;
    funny, though studious ; *"Used'ta have a bike*
    named Red Squirrel", I'd say ; Janine ; oaken
    creatures of magnificence

stationery, import relative cross-thought to paper, as
    if stone, and then as if stone has never been,
    and then as goodness in the binding fetch of
    thousands of interiors who will find it in a
    moment to be true

streamside, IT WAS THERE & IT WAS ..

stringency, see *Staunchness*, also, *Reluctance*,
    Manifestation, & *Pine Needle* **sun.**

swimble, see *squimble*

swizzle, COVERLET (QUAM PRIMUM)

syllables (or windows, number of), *as conceivably*
   relative a pre- or post- runner to
   "*55*" of ˋTen Control Millsˋ (2016) ; see also
   Rilke, R. (1922, cycle) ;

653-30 The Palace of Fifty-five
Windows, built in 1427,
Bhadgaon

NEPAL AND THE HIMALAYAS
(350-653)
Photographed by Emil Muench

T

there, IT WAS THERE & IT WAS ..

thing, "*It's happening, the whole.. moon day sun thing..*"
   3, CASKET LEAF

Tillamook, EASY BEFORE HEAL

tomato cactus, *Probably not possible* ; "tomato cans",
   early confusable

tooths, IT WAS THERE & IT WAS .. ; "Entire: *Leaf*
   margins not toothed"

tractor, EASY BEFORE HEAL

triassic (*in* Nova Scotia, Canada), (*Fr.*) viz. "Le rocher
en equilibre"; *cf.* essential interlude for Flute§
of the Leafcutter, as would become or beckon
within this text; post-ferry, a Sunday perhaps.
Wait, no, it was Wednesday; or Thursday.

two-*l*, *Irreferenceable though referenced once*

U

umbrella, SETTLING OF MAKER'S HANDS

uncracked, LIFELIKE

us, ORANGE

V

vale, *see* poems or other viable constructions in this
text which either refer to, denote or take
place within or amongst lowlands, not
excepting bogs

veins, SKIN

verlaine, *none though it is sometimes*

vigesimal *(base 20)*, there is poem using this meter

vinculum, *over SQUARESLS, beyond "Trapezius"*

violin (not playing) (silence of), *continuous not-playing,*
or silence of

violist(s), *2013*

visto, "*from this book itself*: some of the patterns herein
assimilate (particularly the
interludes, and even if not interludes
nonetheless exchanges which can occur as a
certain period of rest that identifies
horizontally across primary movements), to
things, like, closer an 'andante' attempted in
the project "Ten Control Mills", whether
active in the first of its sections (as ostensibly
named), or, from that foundation, when the
section's intention yields fact to later stage in
promises that grow into the end of the book .

W
(the) way [that] when you hang on something, *you
plan*
           to land on your left foot ; or right!
"[by] w", *unforeseen circumstance* (either title or
           semi-interlude page)
what were thought to be pine needles, *A morning in ..*
which, (also an entry now), *a single branch was extracted
           from a hallway into an outside corridor, fascicle
           after fascicle, many of them at once, at the slightest
           brush made small mazes on falling to the floor*

wild, *One was just waiting for oneself to be let by oneself*
        into
"wist", invented phrase (*cf.* CUPOLA), perhaps the
        sound aback the instrument an oud
"with regard to" (*or*, as can have convention to be
        abbreviated ("w\r\t"), /   /   /   .. /
        Potentially vastly different in intent as component
        of initiator to new language event from "to
        inquire" *albeit not absently dissimilar in*
        functional preference or curiosity, whether in a
        roundabout way or in tract lighted well to the
        originating idea or nodule of thought,
        pre-thought, end-thought, etc., & on a free plane,
        within which the former is some variable a, *and*
        latter b, *whereby a common predecessor may be*
        arranged like, using either (`` I am writing _ ``
)(*I am writing w\r\t ; I am writing t \ i*), *it seems*
        either could perhaps have the undoubted
        preference of a question, though b *is only a query,*
        and a, *as it happens to stand in time, has some*
        knowledge or preceded observable growth that
        whether actual or invented is a basis to the
        receiver on which any kind of voluntary or
        involuntary response would be formed and
        elicited; besides the possibility of invention, if we

take the position of each as a circle of reference
anyhow, for instance *that they would be unique*
and neither overlapping (or outspinning [cf.
OUTSPINNING]*), and both not conceivably*
arranged in a cross-form yielding several
available points of glue making one idiom brighter
than the other, and forgiving whether any is used
a certain way, under some circumstance, or
circumlocution or another, or another, or another,
or, **or,**

wheel, COVERLET 0

wonder, "I have dreams that she believes I become
her."

wrinkle, CASKET LEAF

Y

"[by] y", *unforeseen circumstance* (either title or
semi-interlude page)

yesterday, NEW GREETING, AND SQUIRRL'S
MOON ; A, B, Z ; *8 9 12*

X

"[by] x", *unforeseen circumstance* (either title or
semi-interlude page)

xenon, *see Franklin*✱ (an early electronic utensil,

language by digit, caw by un-caw,
consideration by lookup, re-articulation by
looking guard, cartoon by quorum, learning
by learning, grasps by bats, contiguations by
glass, logic within logic, within logic,
accompanied by a pan-continuous
duo-blocked word game `Word Train`.

zookeeper(*s*), COVERLET (*QUAM* PRIMUM)

�ง

E.

{   i   p

o   l

e   g   ▰

On a secret trail where I sit.

GHOST **MINT**

In the examining of a zone
Behind a swelling lake

It liked to prepare mint,
Roasted of fire, a fern
Nearly always stood by,
Small brine sat in a sallow
Glass, though risen

And an offering to
The air itself.

An edge bent wanted to
Get out. By a new
Manifesting of sound,
It did.

Beeswax poured from the stars,

and Mars rose suddenly !

Whims of the past
Come anew, jolts over
Grave wire sentineled comedy
To old office and office in garages,
Where earlier that
Evening an air comp-
Ressor had busted.

Bingo ran around in
The field. Kismet
Watched. The sun
Rang around the
Rhododendrons in
The morning. We

All offered toasted mint
To the ghost.

There's a
sideways fire

and butterfly wire,

rock with a snake
legend and
crowshaken clave

FROZEN TRANSFER

Everyday
      tired

Everyday
      tried

Everyday
      "rited"

S. V.

The epilogue is a forest beyond the forest.

We love you.

IT WAS THERE & IT WAS THERE

Listen. It's as on a cut surface, tooths
       Listen. Is there noise, who dusk's blouse
       looks up on maps where for ages
       lost were days
       of song mixed with forest
       and sparrow playing overhanging roots
       streamside, clay bakes beneath wavering
       routes of flying insects, burgundy
       petunias and midsummer lime roost
       in the nostrils of elk
       and in the tendentiousness of gnats

       There causes for nothing to be, and the desks
       of frogs note passing registers of oboe-like
       ruminations perhaps sent for them, or other
       shared windwise by drifting heat
       and potent

copies of glimmering morphous bog beat. There
thanks the dancing knotweed, We will make night
our twine. The beards of bristled rocks and legs of limber
lichen kissed ants and sure scaffolds of lichen
licked and greeted new lichen, while
moths beset tiny eggs in
twin pairings before morning-found
methods' eyes float on
leaves near-dry, reguiding
color to their form and
swivels, evincing voices
over leaflings, washing pebbles
and rodent's tufts in the ears
and fixing bended manes
on newly suckl'd time, though
any moon would make
a new moon's day.

When all of life washes over you
The trees make the disappearing sun
Gleam its final truth

who viewed

the index an active

poem, or play, or dance.

H

A F

L M

   O D S

   O A *U*

   N Y N

H

A F

L M

   O D S

   O A U

   N Y

Joshua Lickteig was born in Wisconsin
in 1983. This is his third book of poetry.
In the Belling Stillness, Ten Control Mills
He lives in Portland, Oregon.

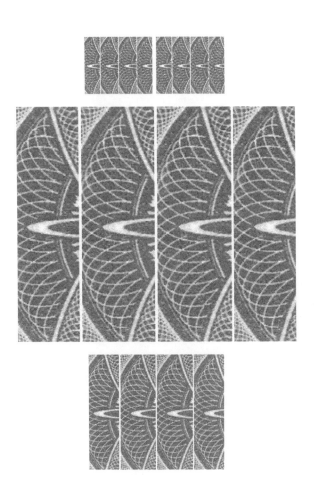

Libre Baskerville, the typeface as font in this book, is a serif. Known as a *transitional*, its family began around the middle 1700's, at the time set by metal punchcutters. Rather than most serifs it has clear, for most characters, curvilinear terminals.

Made in the USA
Middletown, DE
16 October 2023